DRAW MANGA STYLE

KAWAii CUTiES

A beginner's step-by-step guide for drawing super-cute characters

ILARIA RANAURO

QUARRY

CONTENTS

INTRODUCTION

Hello, everyone! My name is Ilaria Ranauro. On the Internet, I'm known as ilariapops. After studying graphic design and pursuing a career as a designer, I quit my day job in 2017 to start a journey as an illustrator. I've always been passionate about drawing, especially cute characters, so when I became unhappy with my job, I decided I should at least give a career as an illustrator a try. So I did!

I'm self-taught, so it took me quite a while to find my style and understand which mediums were the right ones for me. As I share in this book, when you decide that you want to learn how to draw, you need to establish a practice that includes three things: observing other artists' work, creating a routine that lets you draw every day, and allowing yourself the time to make ugly art so you can experiment and improve!

Here's a little bit about my process. I start by brainstorming about the kind of character I want to create. Is it an animal, an object, or a person? I also write down a short list of words that describe how I'd like the character to look and its personality. Then, I take my pencils and sketchbook and start making some drawings. I pick the one I like the most, digitize it, and then work on it on my iPad to finalize my illustration.

I hope this book will ignite your curiosity and teach you about the kawaii style, inspire you to create your own characters, and help you develop a love of drawing.

Let's get started!

HOW TO USE THIS BOOK

Kawaii Cuties presents step-by-step lessons to help you learn about this fun style. The book is divided into two main parts:

Kawaii Essentials. The first section presents tutorials on drawing kawaii characters, including body proportions, facial expressions, and character options, developing your own unique style, and kawaii-style tips and tricks.

Kawaii Characters, Step by Step. This section includes adorable character tutorials, from animals to people. Each character has simple step-by-step illustrations so you can learn the process and start drawing right away.

Have fun drawing kawaii style!

GETTING STARTED WITH KAWAII

WHAT IS KAWAII?

The word *kawaii* originally derives from the Japanese phrase *kao hayushi* (顔映し), meaning "(one's) face (is) aglow," which is commonly used to refer to the blushing or reddening of the face. Kawaii is roughly translated as "cute" and describes the adorable physical features that children and baby animals have. Kawaii things are usually soft, round, and small. They give you happiness and make you smile.

The concept of kawaii began as a rebellion against traditional Japanese culture in the 1970s. Girls started to write, draw, and adopt a cuter style of dressing to counter the roles that society wanted them to have. This cultural revolution permeated the art world, including the visual arts, performing arts, fashion, and music.

In the mid-70s, when Japan entered the Bubble Economy era, companies such as Sanrio started to create kawaii products. The boom of the kawaii culture began in 1974 when Hello Kitty was born. The success of this loveable cat with a red ribbon and almost no expression led to the realization that if you made something cute, it would sell. As a result, various companies started to manufacture goods that were simple but charming. Kawaii is not only found in illustration and merchandising, but it is also present in music, fashion, and even food.

Kawaii characters are a very powerful communication tool and are used for billboards, on posters in train stations and on the streets, and to make advertising flyers with the aim of explaining or selling something.

But what makes something look kawaii? Kawaii characters usually have a big head, very round and tender eyes, pink cheeks, and pastel colors, although these traits are not all mandatory.

It's common to find humans or animals with kawaii features, but inanimate objects can also be converted into characters that move and express feelings.

In fact, you only need a few lines to draw a really cute character. Kawaii art is all about simplification. This is what I like the most about kawaii. There is no limit to your imagination and literally any object can be turned into a character. You can use as many subjects as you like, and people will smile and have fun with them. Add a face to the illustration of a muffin or draw a juice box winking, and you will already be creating kawaii art!

DRAWING TOOLS

You don't need to invest in a lot of tools when you are just starting to draw kawaii doodles. All you need is paper and a pencil; or you can draw digitally on a portable tablet, also called a pen display or pen tablet. To transfer your sketches from the paper to the tablet and to color them digitally, you only need to scan them or take a photo.

Don't be discouraged if you don't have fancy equipment at the beginning. Over time, you will discover what tool you like the most, and you can start thinking about investing more on that.

Even though I am a digital artist, I love to sketch on paper because I don't want to lose the enjoyable feeling of using traditional tools. It's also a good excuse to purchase new arts and crafts supplies from time to time!

Sketchbooks. My favorite sketchbook size is the larger A4 because it gives me more room to draw on a single page. In my opinion, a sketchbook with a soft cover is better because it is lighter, which is something to think about if you want to bring it with you and carry it in your backpack. I am not too picky when it comes to the type of sketchbook paper because I mainly use pencils, but if you want to use markers or watercolors, then look for a paper weight in the 100 to 140 lb (150 to 300 gsm) range.

Pencils. For sketching, I love to use the Edelweiss HB black pencil from Caran d'Ache because the lines come out smooth, it's super easy to erase, and doesn't smudge so you don't get dirty after using it for a while. Recently, I discovered mechanical pencils, and my favorites are the 0.7 mm Pilot Color Eno, as they come in different colors. They are great because they are erasable, and if you decide to color in your drawing afterward, the sketching lines are less visible than those made by classic black pencils.

Erasers. My favorite erasers are the so-called "dust-free" erasers because as the name suggests, they don't make too much dust, and it's nice to keep your working space clean while you draw.

Markers and Colored Pencils. When I color my sketches, I prefer to use colored pencils. There are hundreds of sets on the market, for all levels of artists from beginners to professional. For art markers, I like to use acrylic markers, such as uni POSCA, for a vibrant effect or alcohol markers, such as Copic markers, which allow me to color with layers and gradients. Sometimes, I even like to mix the media, so I start coloring with pencils and then add details or strokes with markers.

Procreate App. As a digital artist, the tool that I use the most is Procreate. This is without a doubt the most popular digital painting and illustration drawing app for the iPad. It is not free, but the price to download the app is affordable. Procreate is a complete art studio that you can take anywhere. It is packed with unique features and has many intuitive creative tools. You can use it to make drawings and even animations, and since you can import new brushes into Procreate, there is no limit in terms of drawing styles.

Procreate is straightforward and easy to use. There are also many tutorials available online.

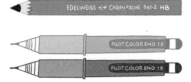

PROPORTIONS

In kawaii culture, a common rule is to draw a big head and a round body. These features are going to give a childlike, sweet, and irresistible look to our character. The proportion of the body in kawaii style is very different from the traditional way of drawing a human or animal body.

There are four figure proportion ratios you can use when you want to draw a kawaii character.

1. THE 50/50 PROPORTION

Draw a square and divide it into two equal parts, so that 50 percent of the space is used for the head and the other 50 percent for the rest of the body.

Of course, these are not exact percentages. It only means that the amount of space taken by the head is the same as the amount of space taken by the body. Now, you have enough room to add details. For example, you can give your character a more lavish outfit and also work on the facial expression and the position of the body.

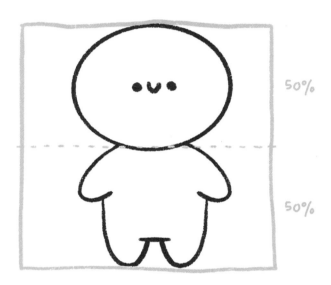

2. THE 60/40 PROPORTION

The square is now divided into two slightly uneven parts so that you have a bigger head and a smaller body. Adding a few more lines will be enough for drawing the body if you don't want to give your character a detailed outfit.

This proportion is also commonly used to draw animals. In fact, the head is the feature that tells you the most about the animal. You only need to add two rounded ears to make a bear or two big eyes to make a frog, and it will be immediately recognizable.

3. THE 70/30 PROPORTION

Some kawaii artists like to exaggerate these proportions even more and draw a huge head on their characters.

So, if you divide the square so that 70 percent is for the head and 30 percent is for the body, you are going to have a very big head and a tiny little body.

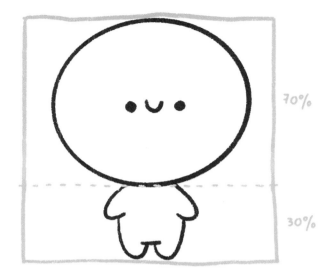

4. THE 100 PERCENT PROPORTION

With this proportion, the character is going to be undivided, meaning you can't distinguish the head from the body. These are the characters that are usually more creative and original. The most famous examples are Molang and Piu Piu from the popular TV show or Pusheen from social media. This proportion is also the one used to draw inanimate objects, such as an avocado or a mug. Just adding a simple facial expression will turn that object into a charming kawaii character.

DRAWING KAWAII: HUMAN CHARACTERS

I know that drawing people might sound intimidating, but you don't need anatomy lessons in order to start practicing. Use references such as pictures or look at yourself in a mirror. You can even take a picture of yourself in a particular position. I do that all the time!

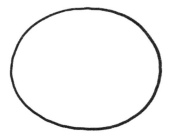

Let's start with the face. Draw a circle, making it a little squashed.

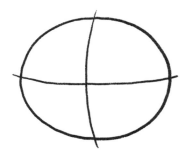

Divide the circle with perpendicular lines, like this.

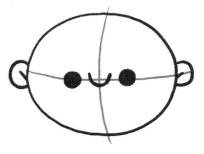

These guidelines will help you position the eyes, mouth, and ears of your character.

The body doesn't have to be detailed at the beginning.

Move the position of the face to have the body appear less static. You can always draw in the guidelines if you need direction.

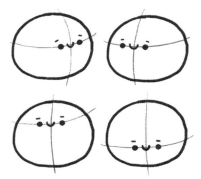

See how the face changes when the character looks right or left and up or down?

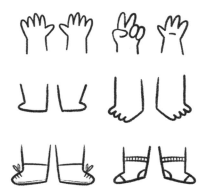

Hands and feet can be as simple or as detailed as you like. Remember to make them slightly curved in order to give a childlike tone to your illustration. Your character can even have four fingers or toes if that's what you prefer. It doesn't have to be realistic. It can be as cartoonish as you like!

Play around with the position of the body. Your character can sit down, run, lay on one side, or dance! If you don't feel confident with a position right away, first draw in some light lines and then add the details. Focus on the overall movement. Don't worry if your drawings aren't perfect.

TIPS

Here are some things that you can try out while drawing a human character:

- Draw one character with glasses.
- Add cheeks and other details, such as eyebrows, a nose, or freckles.

When you draw the hair, remember that you need to add some volume on top of the circle of the head. Kawaii hairstyles are similar to manga hairstyles, but kawaii hair doesn't look three-dimensional. It looks like a flat shape. Unlike realistic hair, for which you use a broken outline to show hair overlap, separate clumps of hair, and single strands, the kawaii hair outline goes all around the head in one smooth continuous line. Remember that you can use fun colors. The hair can be pastel pink, purple, or green, making your character look even cuter and 100 percent kawaii!

DRAWING KAWAII: ANIMAL CHARACTERS

There are three options for drawing kawaii animals.

OPTION 1: 50:50 PROPORTION IN A STANDING POSE

In this example, we draw a raccoon standing up so it looks like a little person.

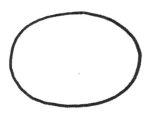

1. Start by drawing the head.

2. Using the 50:50 proportion, add the body and the tail.

TIPS

- You can exaggerate some details; for example, making the ears bigger or drawing the shapes rounder, to enhance the kawaii mood.

- You can even dress your animal like a human to make it look even more delightful and give it more character.

3. Add all the details. You can also add cheeks and a puff of hair to make it look more kawaii.

OPTION 2: NATURAL POSE

In this example, our raccoon is sitting.

1. Always start with the head and then add the body and the details. You can roughly sketch the pose first and then draw over it with a more definitive line to finalize it.

2. Remember that to make your character look kawaii, avoid any style that's too realistic. The animal should be round, have its eyes and nose placed on the same baseline, and can have ridiculous features, such as bushy eyebrows and rosy cheeks.

3. Practice drawing different natural poses. It's okay to use photos for visual reference!

OPTION 3: 100 PERCENT PROPORTION

With this option, you draw a single round shape that includes all the animal's distinguishing characteristics.

This shape makes your character look really loveable and comical, but it also limits the range of movement and attainable poses.

This proportion is a perfect fit for animals with small legs or insects that have a big body and tiny legs. The more compactly they're drawn, the more adorable they look. To draw a ladybug, for example, make an oval shape that includes its essential features: a red body with black dots, antennae, legs, and so on. Then, you only need to add a cute face to complete the kawaii style.

DRAWING KAWAII: OBJECT CHARACTERS

Drawing kawaii objects is really fun because there's essentially no limit to what you can draw. You can choose even the most boring subject and still transform it into an adorable character!

In order to find inspiration, look at the objects that surround you or that you use on a daily basis. You can go out for a walk and take pictures of some of the items that you find while window shopping or just get inspired by nature, observing the flowers or other foliage that's in season.

Let's start by drawing a milk or juice carton. I first draw the shape of the object, using rounded lines, and then add a face. To make it look even more adorable, I add arms, legs, and glowing cheeks!

Practice drawing different facial expressions by sketching the same object over and over. Try several combinations: move the position of the face, add distance between eyes and mouth, draw a nose, glasses, or happy eyes, and so on!

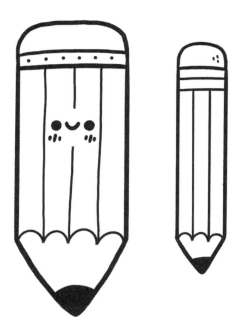

Remember that you need enough space to be able to add a facial expression, so draw your objects a little wider than their real-world counterparts, especially when you draw thin objects, such as pens, carrots, or bottles. This will make them look chubby and lovable.

HELLO!

Finally, embellish your character with speech bubbles, ribbons, stars, hearts, a little bowtie, and so on.

In order to practice with objects, pick a category or a group of items that belong together and start drawing.

Try drawing fruit, vegetables, snacks, Japanese food, cups, plants, and stationery, or you can empty your bag and draw everything that's inside it in a kawaii style. Have fun by practicing!

FACIAL EXPRESSIONS

The most simple and common way to create kawaii expressions is to draw two dots for the eyes and a semicircle for the mouth. What gives your character the cutest expression is aligning the eyes and the mouth on the same baseline.

Varying the distance between the eyes and the mouth can change the appearance of a facial expression, so go ahead and make some trials. Do not settle for the first attempt. Try more than one combination to see which one is best for your character. The most famous kawaii characters, such as Hello Kitty, always have the same expression. The personality of a character can also be expressed with movement, their body, or the environment.

Some character's expressions are very simple, but you can add more details, such as cheeks, eyebrows, tiny noses, little puffs of hair, and so on.

In order to practice facial expressions, search for "facial expressions ideas" on Pinterest or another large image bank and use the pictures as a reference.

FINDING YOUR OWN STYLE

If you are reading this book, I'm guessing that you want to improve your drawing skills or maybe develop a career as an illustrator. But even if you want to draw just for fun, you need to find your style!

Having a style means that you draw in a distinctive, individual way that is specific to you. A unique style will make your work recognizable, and it will help you to stand out.

The process of developing a style can take some time, so be patient! Personally, it took me more than a year to find a style that I was comfortable drawing, and I really don't think that I will remain with this exact style forever.

A style can change over time, and it improves with practice.

Let's explore some ideas that can help you along this journey.

Here's an older drawing of mine (left) from 2018 compared to a more recent one (right). Can you see how my style has changed?

LOOK AT OTHER ARTISTS' WORK

In order to understand what you like, you need to look at other artists' works. Visit your favorite bookstore, go to the children's books or graphic novels section, and go through as many books as possible. You can even buy the ones you like the most and build a small collection that will come in handy as an inspiration source.

Find illustrations on Pinterest and make a collection. You can do the same with Instagram, following the illustrators that speak to you the most. After a while, you will have a better understanding of what you like because the styles, the color palettes, and the techniques will start to appear repeatedly.

If you want to work in this industry, the process of observing the expertise of other artists can also help you understand the field you want to pursue. As I always loved cute characters, it was clear to me that a simple, childish style was the one to go with and that the field that suited me the most was young children's books and merchandising.

BUY THAT SKETCHBOOK AND START TO DRAW!

I know this might sound intimidating, but you need to start drawing, and you need to do it regularly in order to improve. Look at what features you like the most from each of your favorite illustrators and try to merge and mix them to come up with your own way of drawing. Maybe you like how that illustrator draws hair, then you pick the method of drawing eyes from another one, use the color palette from another, and so on.

Remember to look at other artists' work only for inspiration and not to copy their styles.

You can duplicate another artist's drawing only for personal practice. By replicating the illustration, you can learn how the lines come together and how your pencil needs to move in order to draw that style. But leave these attempts exclusively in your sketchbook. Don't post or share them online or claim them as your own.

FIND YOUR FAVORITE MEDIUMS

So, you know that you want to draw. Now the question is, what mediums do you like the most and want to use to create your artwork? If you don't know yet, try exploring your favorite techniques. It could be watercolors, markers, colored pencils, or gouache, or you might find it more convenient to draw on a digital device.

At first, your drawings may look weird, but be gentle with yourself because you are still learning and experimenting. At some point, you will start to like what you draw, and it will feel so good! It is only by practicing that you can fix errant lines, get a true understanding of what features you want to include in your style, and learn what vehicle you feel most comfortable with.

KAWAII STYLE TIPS AND TRICKS

There isn't really a trade secret to finding your style. The key for success is to practice, practice, and then practice even more! Take your time, and don't expect it to happen overnight.

At the beginning, I wasn't used to drawing every day, so I didn't because it didn't feel natural to me. Nowadays, I can't go one single day without drawing something. I still remember the illustrations I was most proud of. They were the ones that made me think that I was improving. Now when I look back, I find them really sweet, and I can recognize how I've grown as an artist since then.

Here are some ideas to help you stay motivated to practice:

- Make fan art. Do you like Harry Potter or Sanrio characters? Redraw them in your style. If you are a complete beginner, then copying other artist's styles can be useful for educational purposes. Remember to keep the drawings to yourself for reference or credit the artist it belongs to if you post on social media.

- Take part in drawing challenges (look for the hashtag #drawthisinyourstyle). You can find many of them on Instagram or Pinterest. They appear as lists of prompts that you can follow for sketching a new drawing every day. You can also create your own list or come up with a project for which you commit to drawing a single subject for a month or even 100 days! I once did a 100 Days of Cute Cats Project for which I drew a cat every day for 100 days. It turned out to be really fun.

If you feel that you need to improve a particular facet—for example, you don't know how to draw dogs or flowers or children—start looking at pictures and draw, draw, draw! There's no way you'll improve if you don't practice and sometimes step out of your comfort zone.

Publish your drawings to get feedback and to keep track of your improvements.

The best way to go is to open an Instagram account and start posting your drawings. Don't be scared! Your followers will love to follow your progress and critique your artwork. You can learn a lot from them.

Finally, a consistent style is what makes an artist stand out and takes their career to the next level. Don't worry if you can't decide and you want to have more than one style. You could think about using them all to fill different niches!

PANDA

4

TIP: Don't feel like you need to be stuck to your initial rough plan—your character's pose, expression, and other elements can evolve as you move through the workflow of a piece.

ALTERNATIVE SKETCHES

Sleepy panda (left) and panda snacking on bamboo (right).

FOX

TIP: Use the body shape as a base and then draw all the details and the final shape over it.

5

ALTERNATIVE SKETCH

Thirsty fox.

RABBIT

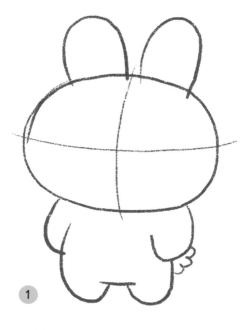

1

2

TIP: You can draw perpendicular lines to help position the face.

3

4

5

ALTERNATIVE SKETCH
Sleepy bunny.

6

CAT

TIP: Draw the cat with a classic shape as well. If you use the trick of putting the eyes and the mouth on the same baseline, it is going to look super-cute!

5

6

ALTERNATIVE SKETCH
Chubby sitting cat.

DOG

(4)

ALTERNATIVE SKETCHES

Sleepy dog (left) and doggy wants a hug (right).

ALPACA

TIP: Use some wavy lines to draw the fleece of the alpaca. This will make it look even cuddlier.

BEE

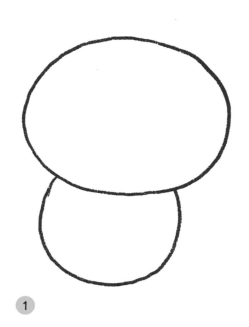

1

2

3

4

ALTERNATIVE SKETCH

Bee flying around flowers.

1

> **TIP:** You can add some flowers and clouds to give an indication of the character's environment.

2

BEAR

1

2

PENGUiN

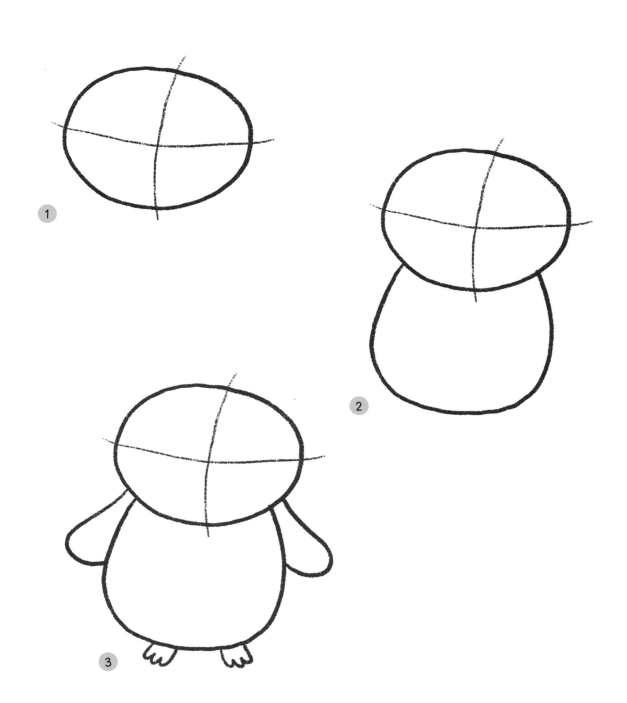

ALTERNATIVE SKETCH

Happy penguin with scarf.

LiON

5

ALTERNATIVE SKETCH
Sitting lion.

TORTOISE

1

2

3

1

2

3

RACCOON

5

ALTERNATIVE SKETCH

Raccoon on all fours.

KOALA

TIP: When you draw an animal from a reference picture, try to extract only a few details, to make it look less realistic and more kawaii.

BiRD

TIP: A bird shape can be as simple as a bean shape!

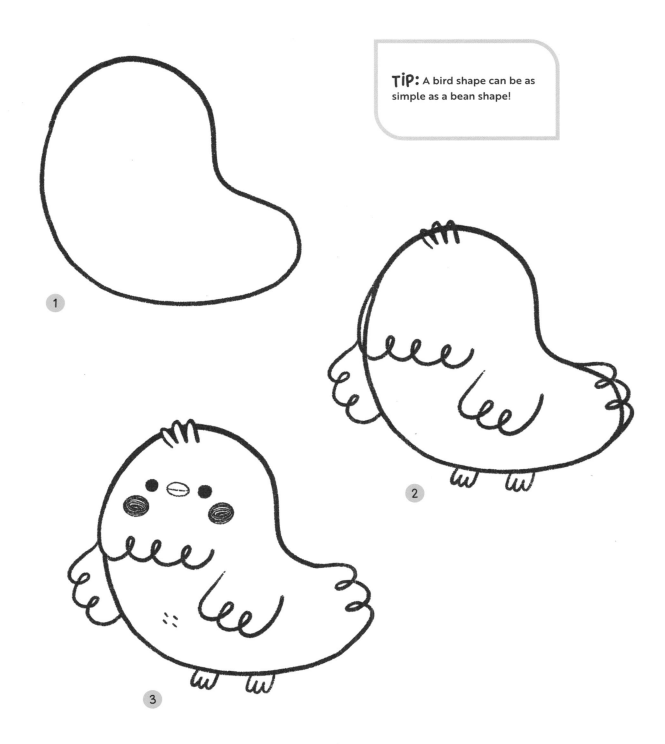

BOY

5

6

ALTERNATIVE SKETCH

More boy faces.

TIP: Experiment with different facial features and haircuts.

GIRL

(5)

ALTERNATIVE SKETCH
More girl faces.

TIP: Try out different facial expressions and hairstyles.

EXPLORER

1

2

3

4

5

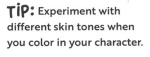

TIP: Experiment with
different skin tones when
you color in your character.

6

ASTRONAUT

5

ALTERNATIVE SKETCH

Astronaut floating in space.

TIP: Add small details, such as little stars or a half moon, around the character to illustrate the surroundings.

COOK

TIP: Pay attention to the outfit. This is what builds your character's identity.

ALTERNATIVE SKETCH

Cook rolling out dough.

4

GARDENER

5

TIP: Have fun drawing some handy tools for your character.

6

SUPERHERO

TIP: Fantasy characters can be very fun to draw. With a superhero, you have endless options for experimenting with colors and shapes.

⑤

ALTERNATIVE SKETCH
Superhero flying.

KiMONO GiRL

TIP: Sometimes, a character requires you to study different cultures. For example, you might need to use picture references to know how to properly decorate a Kimono.

5

6

PAINTER

5

ABOUT THE AUTHOR

Kawaii illustrator **Ilaria Ranauro** (a.k.a. **ilariapops**) sells stickers, washi tape, prints, and other products adorned with her fun images on her popular Etsy shop. She has also illustrated children's books for Penguin Random House Groupo Editorial México. A native of Italy, she is based in Berlin, Germany.

Quarto.com

This library edition published in 2024 by Quarry Books, an imprint of The Quarto Group.
100 Cummings Center, Suite 265-D, Beverly, MA 01915, USA.
T (978) 282-9590 F (978) 283-2742

Distributed in the United States and Canada by
Lerner Publisher Services
241 First Avenue North
Minneapolis, MN 55401 U.S.A.
www.lernerbooks.com

First Library Edition

Library of Congress Cataloging-in-Publication Control Number: 2023039453

Design and Page Layout: Megan Jones Design
Illustrations: Ilaria Ranauro

Printed in USA
10 9 8 7 6 5 4 3